**THE PARISH CHURCH OF ST GILES, WREXHAM** is one ⸋ examples of ecclesiastical architecture to be found in Wales. The ⸋ of the church was built at the end of the 15th and beginning ⸋ centuries, spanning the final years of the medieval period and the ⸋ decades of the modern age.

There may well have been a church in Wrexham as far back as ⸋ century and the present church is probably the third to have been ⸋ the site. Local legend has it that work on building a church was ori ⸋ commenced on what is now Brynyffynnon but that each day's work was destroyed during the night. A watch was kept one night and, as the day's work collapsed, a voice was heard crying 'Bryn-y-grog' (the Hill of the Cross) and it was taken as a divine indication that the church should be built a few hundred yards away on the hill of that name.

Wrexham historian, A.N. Palmer, stated that the earliest reference which he was able to find to a church in Wrexham was 1220 when Reyner, the bishop of St Asaph, gave the monks of Valle Crucis in Llangollen 'half of the [income of the] Church' of the town of Wrexham (the other half being given to them seven years later by the next bishop, Abraham). In reality what this meant was that the rectorial tithe income from the church was given to Valle Crucis. In 1247, Madog ap Gruffydd, Prince of Powys, bestowed upon the monks of Valle Crucis the patronage of the church of Wrexham which meant that the abbey also received the vicar's tithes.

On 25 November, 1330, the church tower (often referred to as a steeple) was blown down, the result of which was that the whole church was rebuilt in the Decorated style. Some features of this 14th century church have survived and formed the basis of the outline of the nave and aisles of the 15th century building. Many believed that this catastrophe had befallen the tower because the market was being held on a Sunday. Consequently, market day was moved to a Thursday. The church is dedicated to St Giles although there is a strong local belief that it was once dedicated to the Celtic saint Silyn. This may, however, have been an error of translation in that both Silyn and Giles can be translated into Latin as Aegidius. It may also be an indication that the origin of the church dates back to the time when Welsh churches were dedicated to Celtic saints, many of whom (Silyn included) were not recognised by the Roman Catholic church. Many churches in the Marches therefore adopted the name of a more legitimate patron. Certainly, by 1494 the church was known as 'the church of Saint Giles'.

## The 15th & 16th Centuries

The 15th century was a period of great political and social unrest in

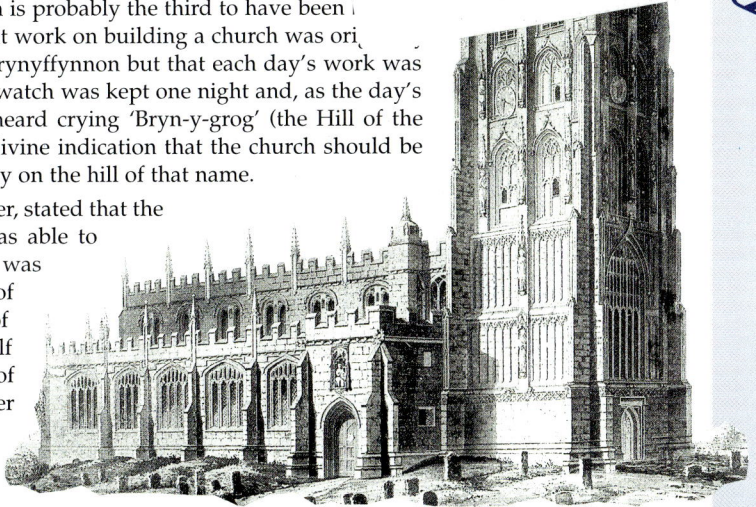

### St Giles

*A 6th or 8th century Athenian who fled to France, Giles lived as a hermit in the Rhône valley. One day, Flavius Wamba, king of the Visigoths was hunting in the nearby forest and gave chase to a hind. The frightened animal fled into a cave where Giles was living and the hermit came forward to protect it and, in doing so, was hit by an arrow meant for the hind. The king, impressed by the hermit's courage and holiness, decided to build a monastery and Giles became its first abbot. It was also said that he had prayed to God that the arrow wound would not be healed saying that 'My strength is made perfect in weakness'. The relics of St Giles are in a shrine in the church of St Sernin, Toulouse, France.*

*St Giles was the patron saint of cripples, beggars and blacksmiths and over 160 churches in Britain are dedicated to him including St Giles, Cripplegate, London and St Giles Cathedral, Edinburgh.*

both Wales and England. The century had started with the rebellion of Owain Glyndwr which lasted with varying levels of intensity until 1415. Perhaps of greater significance as far as Wrexham was concerned, was the economic turmoil which was left in the wake of the uprising and which plunged the principality into an extended period of decline and hardship. At the same time, the struggle for the Crown of England, commonly referred to as the 'Wars of the Roses', brought over 50 years of conflict and instability to almost every corner of the kingdom. By 1461 matters appeared to have been settled in favour of the Yorkist faction headed by Edward IV and 20 years of peace followed.

*A corbel believed to depict the image of Thomas Stanley, 1st Earl of Derby. Why he is shown with the ears of a donkey is unknown.*

In the mid 15th century, either in 1457 or 1463, the Parish Church was gutted by fire and work on the present building was started on the same site a few years later. Some features of the 14th century church were retained, most notably the octagonal pillars and some of the disused corbels which once held up the roof in the easternmost bays of the south aisle.

The first stones of the 15th century Perpendicular style building were supplied by the family of Llwyn Onn, Wrexham. Built of local sandstone, the building has a warm yellow appearance but, sadly, this material is highly susceptible to erosion from the weather and atmospheric chemical pollution. Although this new structure is the core of the present day church, the building was significantly smaller and less richly embellished. The nave and aisles were the same length as today but there was no chancel and no

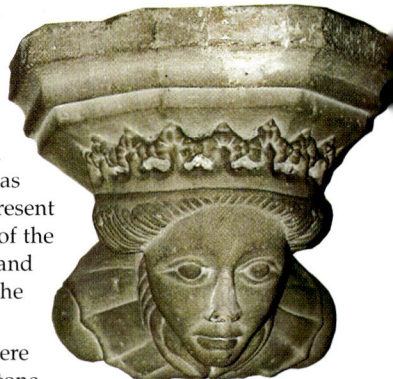

*A corbel believed to depict the image of Lady Margaret Beaufort, Countess of Derby, mother of King Henry VII.*

tower. The building was therefore very much a rectangular shape with a large window behind the altar at the eastern end. The roof was probably quite steeply pitched and rested on the corbels which have survived and can be seen above the piers in the nave. There is, however, some documentary evidence that a wooden *clochty* (bell-tower) was added to the west end of the nave sometime before the end of the century.

By the beginning of the 16th century, the present nave had been completed in the Perpendicular style and extended from the arched entrance to the present chancel to the arched entrance leading to the west tower. In 1506, major works were begun which were to turn a fairly ordinary building into the magnificent structure that we see today. The tower was completed by 1524/5 and, at the same time, the chancel and high altar were added giving the main body of the church an overall length of 54.25m(178ft) and a width of 20.7m (68ft). What prompted such an expensive and wonderful display has gone unrecorded but the heavy Tudor imagery may well provide us with a clue.

In north-east Wales, the Stanley family held sway over large areas of land extending from the Dee estuary in the north to the upper Dee valley in the south. In 1482, Thomas Stanley, 1st Earl of Derby, married Margaret Beaufort, the widowed Countess of Richmond and mother to Henry Tudor (the future King Henry VII). The influence of this family on the Wrexham area, coupled with the accession to the throne of the Tudors in 1485, is evident in the dynastic symbolism which can be seen throughout the Parish Church. This would suggest more than a passing association between the rebuilt church and the newly ascended royal house. Margaret Beaufort was a very devout and philanthropic individual and, as the wife of probably the wealthiest man in England, was in a position to bestow large grants of money upon religious and educational institutions throughout the kingdom, wherever the Stanleys or the Beauforts had strong connections. In north-east Wales, there is considerable evidence of her involvement with the expansion of the churches

## Mason- Marks

*A variety of masons' marks can be found on the stonework both inside and outside the Parish Church. Some are believed to date from the 14th century e.g.*

*And many other mason-marks have been discovered from later dates including:*

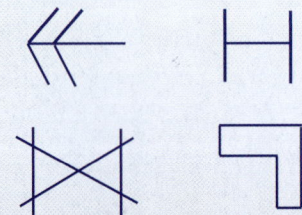

*The chancel viewed from the nave.*

at Mold, Gresford, Holt and the pilgrimage centre of Holywell and, further afield, at Wimbourne Minster in Dorset and Christ College, Cambridge. Located in the most important market town in north Wales, it would have been highly unlikely that the newly constructed church of St Giles would have been omitted from this lady's acts of bounty. Indeed, the elaborate nature of the restructuring of the church in the early 16th century might suggest that St Giles was intended to be the most fortunate of all the parish churches in the area. Unfortunately, Margaret Beaufort died in 1509, shortly after work had begun on the church at Wrexham, and so the direct evidence of her generosity may well have gone unrecorded.

The Tudor Age, opening with the accession to the throne of Henry VII in 1485 and ending with the death of Elizabeth in 1603, is generally viewed as a period of great, almost revolutionary, changes in Britain. Throughout Europe, the Renaissance was making people look at life through new eyes in the fields of science, art, literature and, not least, theology. The Parish Church is Wrexham's Renaissance masterpiece.

The roof was removed from the nave and a clerestory added, followed by a new timber roof with a very shallow pitch. This roof was supported by braces which rested on new corbels placed between the windows in the clerestory. The east window was taken out and a chancel built on the east end. Aisles and a porch were added and work commenced on the great tower at the west end.

The religious upheaval in the 16th century, during the reigns of Henry VIII and Edward VI, meant that St Giles became one of the last major churches to be built before the Reformation. It also meant that the heavy, ornate decoration and imagery so common in medieval churches became a thing of the past and Wrexham's church was decorated in a much more subdued style.

An unconfirmed belief is that St Giles was once either a collegiate church or was considered for collegiate status — a church with a college of priests (canons and prebendaries) instead of a single priest or vicar, and a full range of church services. Leyland wrote in 1537 that the 'goodlie church' of Wrexham was collegiate but had no prebends which would suggest that the process had not been completed. The survival of the names 'College House' (on a building in the churchyard) and College Street and several 'College Farms' in the area would seem to add some weight to the theory. If there is any truth in the story, it would seem likely to have occurred during the 16th century, possibly at the time of the Reformation. Bishop Parfew (1536–55) tried to make the church the centre of the diocese instead of St Asaph and the creation of a collegiate church may have been his idea.

### The 17th Century

Very little was done to the fabric of the church after the early 16th century. One hundred years later, the Puritans had a significant effect upon the internal decoration of the church, but even they did not carry out half the acts of 'vandalism' that are normally associated with them in popular myth. While it is possible that the chancel was screened off from the body of the church and used for secular purposes, the remainder of the building continued to serve Wrexham as a place of worship. Some items were removed, such as the font, but other very 'high church' items, such as the statuary on the exterior of the tower and the Lady Chapel in the south aisle were left in situ. The only recorded acts of deliberate destruction were the removal of the organ and the breaking open of the tomb of Robert ap Iorwerth of Llwyn Onn. During the period of the Interregnum (1649–60) vicars were appointed and included Morgan Llwyd (Lloyd), a native of Merionethshire, who had been educated at Wrexham Grammar School. He had been influenced by Walter Cradoc, a curate in Wrexham and became the Presbyterian vicar of Wrexham during the period of the Commonwealth.

### The 18th and 19th Centuries

At the beginning of the 18th century the Parish Church received a number of gifts from Elihu Yale of Plas Grono, the benefactor of Yale University. Amongst these was a gallery erected to replace the rood-

*The Parish Church from Mount Street, c.1870*
*by Louise Rayner.*
*Courtesy of the Grosvenor Museum, Chester.*

*The interior of the nave c.1825. The newly constructed galleries in the North and South Aisles and the triple-decker pulpit can be clearly seen.*

loft at the eastern end of the nave in 1707. This was moved in 1718 to the west end of the nave. In 1779 an organ was installed for the first time since 1643.

This period brought with it a significant change in the style of worship in Britain. It was an era of rapid expansion for the various Nonconformist denominations and nowhere was this more prevalent than in Wales. All churches began to place greater emphasis upon theology and less upon ceremonial and this more austere view of religion affected even the Anglican Church. In 1819–22 new galleries were erected along both aisles. These, and a triple-decker pulpit, were the focal point of the east end of the nave. Now the sermon was the focus of attention and the additional seating could accommodate the congregation of a rapidly expanding local population.

For the first time, men who had made their fortunes in the local coal, iron and brewing industries became the leading benefactors of the church. A major restoration of both the fabric and furnishings took place in the 1860s and, by the time David Howell was vicar (1876–91), the church was fighting back against the tide of Nonconformity. Of particular significance during the second half of the 19th and early 20th centuries was the breaking up of the ancient parish of Wrexham and the creation of new parishes at Brymbo, Minera, Gwersyllt, Rhostyllen and Rhosddu, and later, daughter churches: St Marks, St John the Baptist's, Dewi Sant, St Michael's (now All Saints) and St Peter's. In the 1890s, a substantial part of the south side of the churchyard was lost when the Wrexham–Ellesmere Railway built a viaduct through it.

## The 20th Century

The 20th century opened with a major restoration programme on the fabric of the building, particularly the tower. This activity continued off and on throughout the century. Declining congregations led to the closure and demolition of several churches (St Mark's, Dewi Sant, St John the Baptist's and St Peter's) but new churches were built in Garden Village, Rhosnesni and Queens Park.

*David Howell, vicar of Wrexham 1875–91 and his Memorial Window depicting a scene from the Sermon on the Mount.*

## The Churchyard

This was once a focal point of the town and the site of the weekly markets. All Anglican burials took place here until 1793 when a new cemetery was opened on Ruthin Road. Amongst those buried here are Elihu Yale of Plas Grono (1649–1721), Sir Roger Palmer of Cefn Park (1832–1910) — Charge of the Light Brigade survivor, and artist John Downman, R.A. (1750–1824). The churchyard was levelled in 1904.

Entry to the churchyard is by way of the wrought iron gates manufactured by local smith Robert Davies of Croesfoel. Erected in 1720, the gates originally sealed off Church Street and were attached to the buildings on either side. In 1807/8 they were moved back and formed part of a new wrought iron railing which surrounded the churchyard. They were moved to their present position in 1820. On the open book above the gates, facing Church Street, are the words: *O go your way into His gates with thanksgiving, and into His courts with praise* [Ps 100:4]. On the reverse, facing the church

*The tomb of Elihu Yale and, just visible on the west wall of the tow the stone removed from the tower at Yale University, US*

and a parting thought for the visitor, are: *Go in peace and sin no more* [John 8:11]. The two gates, side wickets, short screen-lengths and two dimensional piers, were sympathetically restored in 1900.

In the north-west corner of the churchyard stands College House which today houses the Parish Office.

The sun dial located near to the north door was a gift from Edward Ravenscroft in 1809.

*Elihu Yale, courtesy of Yale University, USA.*

### Elihu Yale

*Born in Boston, Massachusetts in 1649, the second son of David Yale, a prosperous merchant and a descendant of the Yales of Plas yn Iâl and Plas Grono, Wrexham. The family returned to Plas Grono in 1651 before settling in London.*

*Elihu went to India in 1671, where he remained until 1699 and had a very successful career including a period as Governor of Fort St George. He returned to London a very wealthy man and spent the last 22 years of his life between Plas Grono and Queens Square, London. He died in London on 8 July 1721 and was buried in Wrexham Parish Churchyard on 22 July.*

*He is best remembered for his generosity to Connecticut College. On 11 June 1718, he sent the college two trunks of textiles which were to be sold at a profit, 417 books, a portrait and the arms of King George I – total value about £1,162. In 1721, he sent the college further goods to the value of £562. As the largest benefactor of the college, the authorities adopted the name Yale College. He also made gifts to many other organisations including Wrexham Parish Church and the Society for the Propagation of the Gospel, and part funding the publication of a Welsh prayer book.*

*His epitaph reads: 'Born in America, in Europe bred, In Africa travell'd and in Asia wed, Where long he liv'd and thriv'd; in London dead. Much good, some ill, he did; so hope all's even And that his soul thro' mercy's gone to Heaven. You that survive and read this tale, take care, For this most certain exit to prepare: Where blest in peace, the actions of the just Smell sweet, and blossom in the silent dust'.*

*The Davies Gates, the entrance to St Giles' Churchyard from Church Street.*

## The North Porch

Entry to the church is via the north porch which faces the main churchyard gates and Church Street. This was built in the 16th century in the Perpendicular style. Above the door is a badly weathered statue of the Virgin and Child. The porch has two storeys and was restored by the alumni of Yale University as part of that college's 1901 bicentenary celebrations. Boards displayed inside the porch record the names of the incumbents. A boss depicting St Giles can be seen in the centre of the vaulted ceiling (by H. A. Prothero, 1901). The porch also contains an ancient wooden parish chest with iron bands and three locks. In 1867, during the major restoration of the church, traces of a wall painting of the crucifixion were found on the wall of the porch above the chest.

Entering the church, the visitor should look on the wall to the right of the door where a fine example of the Royal Arms of Queen Anne can be seen. As the design was only in use between 1707 and 1714, this is comparatively rare and was presented to the church by Elihu Yale in about 1718.

## The Nave

The nave is bounded on the north and south side by arcades of arches in the Decorated style which originally formed part of the 14th century church. These arches come to a much more pronounced point than the later Perpendicular style arches as seen in the majority of the windows. On either side of the nave, above the piers of the arcade are the corbels which once held up the original roof.

*The Royal Arms of Queen Anne (1702-14).*

The decoration on one of these, depicting a mermaid combing her hair, probably dates from the 14th century church but the others were 'renewed' in the 19th century and are decorated with a variety of features including a Norman king, a chalice, a Tudor rose, a portcullis and a fleur de lys. In 1867, plans were made to place a statue on each of these corbels but only three were actually installed, depicting St Augustine (north arcade), St Paul and Moses (south arcade).

The camberbeam wooden roof dates from the 16th century and is supported on corbels sited between the windows in the clerestory. Each corbel is decorated with an armorial shield. The roof is adorned with 16 musical angels: 10 playing cithers (similar to a lute), 1 playing the bagpipes, 1 playing a double pipe, 2 playing harps and 2 playing an unknown instrument. In addition there are several

*The nave and south aisle, looking towards the chancel.*

The wall painting over the arch at the east end of the nave.

angels singing. At the east end of the roof, the small red face depicts the Devil.

*The face of the Devil in the nave roof.*

Perhaps the most important decorative feature of the nave is the early 16th century wall-painting over the arch of the east wall. This depicts the Day of Judgement and shows figures (including two kings and a bishop) wrapped in shrouds rising from their coffins to present themselves before Christ in Majesty flanked by the Virgin Mary and St John. Unfortunately, the head and shoulders of Christ are missing. On the left of the painting, in an area that has badly faded, appears St Peter receiving a group of figures (including kings, queens, bishops, monks and laity) into the gates of Heaven. In the lower right hand section figures can be seen being consumed by the flames of hell. This painting, which was re-discovered in 1867, seems to be a portrayal of Matthew 25, verses 31–35 and 41: *When the Son of Man comes in his glory and all the angels with him, then he will sit on the throne of his glory. All the nations will be gathered before him, and he will separate people one from another as a shepherd separates the sheep from the goats, and he will put the sheep at his right hand and the goats at the left. Then the king will say to those at his right hand, 'Come, you that are blessed by my Father, inherit the kingdom prepared for you from the foundation of the world; Then he will say to those at his left hand, 'You that are accused, depart from me into the eternal fire prepared for the devil and his angels'.* The centre section of this painting is in a much better state of preservation than the two side sections. This would suggest that for a lengthy period of its history, the centre of the painting was concealed. Certainly, during the 17th century there was a statutory requirement for churches to display the Royal Arms in a prominent position. Examination of evidence in other churches of this period (e.g. St Martin's Church, Wareham) would indicate that the centre of

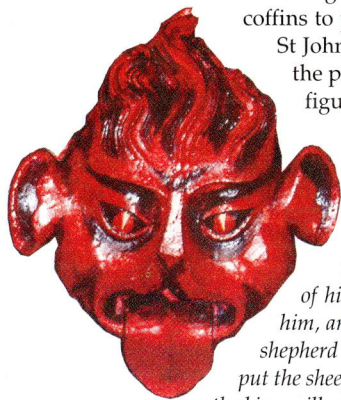

*A roof corbel from the 14th century church.*

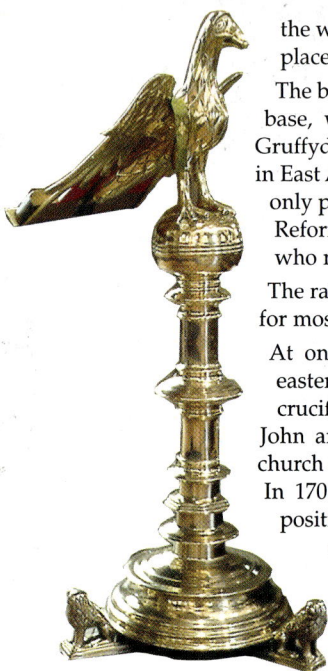

the wall above the chancel arch was the most likely position for the Royal Arms to be placed.

The brass eagle lectern, supported on a moulded stem with three lions decorating the base, was presented to the church in 1524 by Matilda, the daughter of John ap Gruffydd of Plas-y-Stiwart, in accordance with her father's will. It was probably made in East Anglia and cost £6. The law requiring every parish church to provide a Bible was only passed in 1538, and this lectern is one of only about forty surviving from the pre-Reformation period. A study of the lectern's three feet will clearly show that the man who made it had never actually seen a lion.

The raised area at the east end of the nave has an altar which is used for most services.

At one time a rood (wooden) loft existed over the eastern end of the nave and was the location of a crucifix and statues of the Blessed Virgin Mary and St John and, at a later date, it was here that the original church organ was housed. This loft was removed in 1662. In 1707, Elihu Yale had a gallery erected in the same position but eleven years later he paid for it to be moved to the western end of the nave where it remained until 1779.

Box pews were installed in the nave in the 1820s. These were the property of individual members of the congregation and were removed in 1867 and replaced with the present free open pews.

The pulpit is of white Mansfield stone with columns of red Devonshire marble. It was the gift of Peter Walker (Mayor of Wrexham and a local brewer) at the time of the 1867 restoration. The panels are decorated with the figures of Christ and the four evangelists. It was manufactured by Lever of Maidenhead.

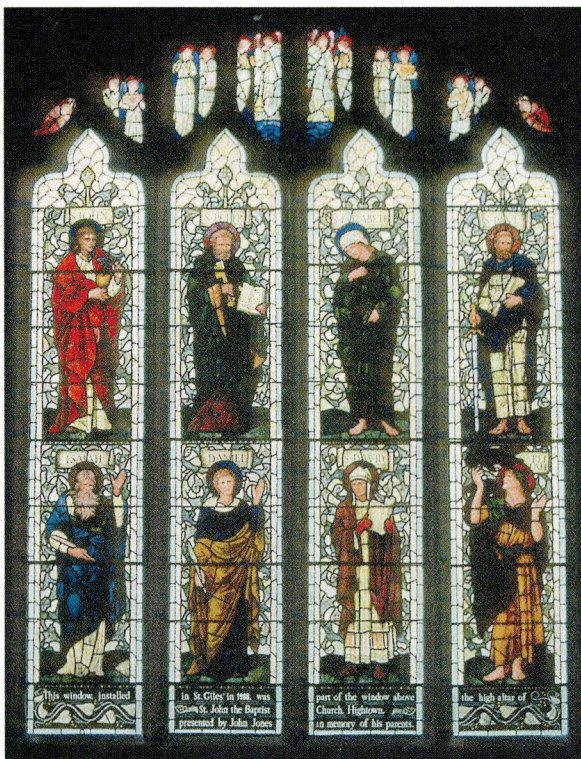

## The North Aisle

This aisle, built in the 15th century, probably on the site of a previous aisle dating back to c.1330, is now the Royal Welch Fusiliers Memorial Chapel and the Wrexham War Memorial Chapel.

Entry to the aisle is by way of the wooden screen presented to the church by the Royal Welch Fusiliers in 1977 and manufactured by John L. Jones & Partners of Cheltenham. This screen originally stood under the west tower but was moved to its present location in the 1980s.

Immediately upon entering the chapel, the visitor will see the Regimental Roll of Honour which records the names of over 10,000 Royal Welch Fusiliers who lost their lives in the two World Wars.

The second window on the left was installed in St Giles in 1988 after the demolition of the Church of St John the Baptist, Hightown, where it had formed part of the window above the high altar. It was designed by the Burne-Jones studio and depicts St John, St Peter, St Elizabeth, St David, St Paul and the prophets Isaiah, Daniel and Elijah. The window was originally presented to St John the Baptist's Church, in

*The St John's Window.*

*The north aisle looking towards the Royal Welch Fusliers Chapel and the War Memorial Chapel.*

memory of his parents, by local brewer John Jones.

Just to the right of the St John's window are carvings of two calvaries (on a step or mound representing the hill of Calvary) and gabled crosses. Their design is unusual and they are believed to be consecration crosses, placed on the building at the time of consecration in the 14th century.

The third window was manufactured by Messrs Powell of London and serves as a memorial window to Bishop Reginald Heber, author of the hymn 'From Greenland's Icy Mountains', whose portrait appears at the bottom right. Designed as a missionary window, each figure depicts a different verse from the hymn.

Between the third and fourth windows is an elaborate sculptured memorial by Louis François Roubiliac (c.1705–62), a French sculptor who became renowned in Britain for his memorials. This memorial is to Miss Mary Myddelton (1688–1747) of Croesnewydd Hall, Wrexham, the daughter of Sir Richard Myddelton, Bt. of Chirk Castle. It was originally located in the chancel but was removed to this position in 1867. The sculpture represents the day of judgement with the angel (top left) blowing his trumpet to summon the dead.

The fourth window was installed to commemorate the tercentenary of the Royal Welch Fusiliers in 1989. Commissioned by the Regiment and designed by Joseph Nuttgens, the window shows men of the RWF in various uniforms from that of 1689 to that of 1989. Also included in the window are the regiment's battle honours and various items of symbolism such as the doves of peace, the Red Dragon of Wales, the Prince of Wales' feathers and the White Horse of Hanover.

To the right of the Royal Welch Fusiliers Tercentenary Window is a decorated corbel. This is believed to date from the 14th century church and depicts a man with a toothache.

The wooden ceiling of the North Aisle dates from the 19th century and has coloured bosses decorated with the symbols of various local organisations e.g. the Borough of Wrexham, Rotary Club, Lions Club, Masonic Lodges, Scouts and Guides.

Hanging from the walls are various colours (flags) belonging to the Royal Welch Fusiliers.

The far end of the North Aisle was originally the Chapel of St Catherine. The dedication to this particular saint may have been inspired by the collapse of the tower in 1330 which took place on St Catherine's day. Certainly, the figure of St Catherine appears on the east face of the present tower, perhaps as a form of protection. There is, however, a second possibility for the adoption of St. Catherine. Much of the decoration of the church

*The Mary Myddelton Memorial.*

took place during the early years of the reign of King Henry VIII. As he married Catherine of Aragon in 1509, it may be that the builders of St Giles chose this saint as a form of tribute to their new queen. Interestingly, one of the figures on the east face of the tower is of an unidentified queen and another is of St James, the patron saint of Spain.

In later years the chapel (or chantry) of St Catherine belonged to the Puleston family of Hafod-y-wern. This was a common practice and a means of paying for the upkeep of different parts of a church. Anyone wishing to make use of such a private chapel had to seek the permission of the owner and, often, had to pay for the privilege. This is the reason why certain memorials in St Giles carry the comment: 'erected with the permission of … …'. Today, this chapel serves as the Wrexham War Memorial Chapel and a marble memorial bearing the names and regiments of each man killed in the First World War can be seen at the far end of the north wall.

Below the War Memorial is the oldest effigy in St Giles. This was found buried in the churchyard at

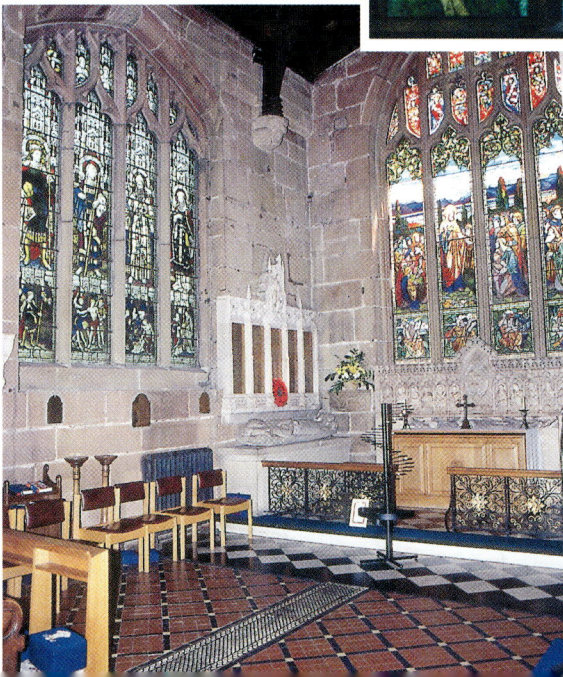

the beginning of the 19th century when digging the foundations for the churchyard gates. Slightly larger than life, it depicts a Welsh knight, bare-headed with long hair. In his right hand he is holding a sword and in his left hand, holds a shield in front of his body. On the shield is a lion rampant and the words HIC JACET KENEVERIKE AP HOVEL [Here lies Cyneurig ap Hywel].

The altar in the War Memorial Chapel is made of wood with an alabaster reredos showing the twelve apostles. Above it is a window depicting the Sermon on the Mount. This was designed by J. Eaddie Reid and made by the Gateshead Stained Glass Co. Ltd of Whitley Bay. The window is a memorial to David Howell, Dean of St. David's Cathedral, who was vicar of Wrexham from 1875–91.

*The chancel seen through the arch created by the removal of the original east window of the nave.*

## The Chancel

The Chancel was built in the 16th century when the east window of the nave was removed. There is ample surviving evidence of this major alteration to the fabric of the Parish Church. The great arch entrance to the chancel was the frame of the east window and at the top, the remains of the original tracery can be seen. On each side of the chancel arch, there are the remains of niches with elaborately carved canopies. Before the removal of the window, these would have extended much lower, possibly to floor level, and would have contained a statue on either side of the altar. On the rear of the chancel arch (which would once have been the outside wall) are the original stepped buttresses that supported the east wall of the church before the chancel was built.

The land on which the chancel was to be built sloped away quite steeply and, in the process of levelling it out, a small crypt was constructed below which served as a vestry and which was reached either by a door to the left of the altar

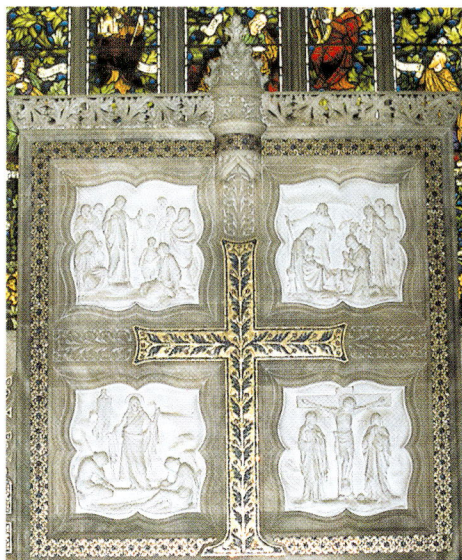

*The central section of the reredos.*

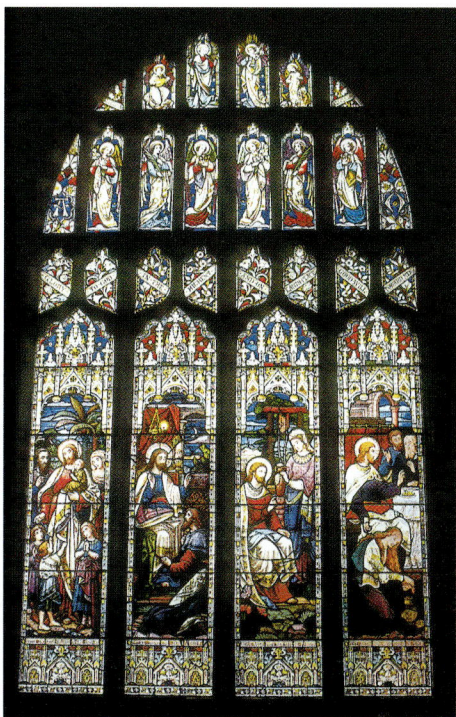

*The Cunliffe Memorial Window.*

or by a door from the churchyard. The chancel underwent a major refurbishment in 1914 under the direction of architect Sir Thomas Graham Jackson of Wimbledon. The chancel itself has a 'polygonal apsidal' (a multi-sided semi-circular) shape with a wooden roof which dates from the 19th century. The entrance to the chancel is marked by a low, wrought-iron screen which was probably presented to the church by Elihu Yale c.1707 and is the work of the father and son smiths, Hugh and Robert Davies of Croesfoel.

The three altar windows were designed by Sir Thomas Jackson in 1914 and executed by James Powell & Son. The east window behind the altar depicts the Jesse Tree and is dedicated to the memory of Sir Robert Egerton. The window immediately to the left of the altar is dedicated to the memory of John Allington Hughes, while the one to the right, behind the choir stalls, is in memory of the Reverend George Cunliffe, vicar of Wrexham 1826–75.

The wooden altar table was carved on three sides by Carlo Scarselli of Florence. It is surmounted by a large reredos which was installed during the 1914 refurbishment and contains four panels depicting scenes from the life of Christ. The earlier wooden reredos is now in Petton Church in Shropshire.

On the south-east wall of the chancel, inside the sanctuary, is an ornate triple sedilia decorated with carved spandrels and heads (some of which depict pagan green men). This dates from the 14th century and was moved to the present chancel from elsewhere in the church. A sedilia of this type

*The sedilia on the south-east wall of the chancel.*

was where the priest, deacon and sub-deacon would sit during services.

Below the Cunliffe Memorial Window is an effigy of Hugh Bellot, bishop of Bangor (1585–95) and Chester (1595–6) who died at Plas Power, Wrexham. He assisted Bishop William Morgan with his masterly translation of the Bible into Welsh. The effigy, although badly damaged, shows Bellot dressed in the post-Reformation attire of a Doctor of Divinity of the University of Cambridge — a scarlet robe (chimere), ermine tippet and a ruff.

On the north wall, just inside the chancel arch is a three-dimensional memorial by Louis Roubiliac to the Reverend Thomas Myddelton (died 1754) and his wife Arabella (died 1756) with portraits of both under a draped canopy. Opposite, on the south wall of the chancel is a marble cartouche memorial to members of the Yale family who died at the end of the 17th century, given by Elihu Yale.

## The South Aisle

Like the north aisle, the south aisle dates mainly from the 15th century although close examination (from the churchyard) of the most easterly window reveals that it is in the Decorated style common in the 14th century. Also, behind the organ, and not visible to the public, is the remains of a piscina, a medieval perforated stone basin used for washing the chalice after the celebration of mass. The eastern end of the aisle was originally the Lady Chapel, dedicated to the Virgin Mary and was in use as such as late at the mid 16th century. This chapel became the property of the Llwyn Onn family and part of it was sold to the Lloyd family of Esclus (Esless) Hall. Concealed behind the organ is a memorial to Sir Richard Lloyd of Esclus Hall who was Governor of Holt Castle and Chief Justice of North Wales during the Civil War. He received King Charles I at Brynyffynnon House in 1642. He died on 5 May 1676 and was buried beneath the south aisle. The chapel now houses the church organ.

*A sketch of the piscinia.*

Five of the windows in this aisle were designed and executed by Charles Eamer Kempe and the firm of Kempe & Tower.

When Dewi Sant (St David's) Wrexham's Welsh church in Rhosddu Road, was closed, the name was transferred to the area to the west of the organ which was dedicated as the Chapel of Dewi Sant. The altar is in memory of W. Noel Soames, a member of the notable Wrexham brewing family.

A blocked doorway located high in the north wall was the entrance to the rood loft.

There are some interesting memorials on the south wall, most notably: a marble tablet in memory of Ann, wife of the famous ironmaster John 'Iron Mad' Wilkinson, owner of the Bersham Ironworks and founder of the Brymbo Ironworks; a decorative brass memorial to Sir Evan Morris, JP, Mayor of Wrexham and a brass plate commemorating those members of the Denbighshire Hussars Imperial Yeomanry who died while serving in South Africa, 1900–02.

On the rear wall of the south aisle is an amusing cartouche memorial:

*Daniel Jones dy'd ye 13th day of Feby, 1668.*
*Here lies interr'd beneath these stones*
*The beard, ye flesh and eke ye bones*
*Of Wrexham Clerk old Daniel Jones.*

## The Ante Nave

The ante nave dates in part from the 14th century but most of what is visible today was built in the early 16th century.

On the south wall is a large marble memorial to Sir Foster Cunliffe, Bt, (died 1834) of Acton Hall, Wrexham, and his wife Harriet (died 1830).

The octagonal stone font is of unknown date, but is known to have been part of the furnishings of the 16th century church. During the period following the Civil War the font disappeared and was not recovered until 1843 when it was found in the garden of Little Acton House. The decorative panels were restored at that time. The font which had been used in the interim period was placed in St James' Church, Rhosddu.

On the north wall hangs a painting by an unknown artist of King David playing a harp. This was a gift to the church from Elihu Yale in about 1718. Below the painting is a memorial to Ellen, wife of Archibald Peel of Marchwiel and daughter of Sir Roger Palmer of Cefn Park. The sculpture shows Ellen being greeted by her infant son, Archibald Roger, who had predeceased her.

Hanging from the north wall is the flag of the United States of America which was presented to the Parish Church by the 129th General Hospital, U.S. Army, in July 1945, a military unit based in Penley during the Second World War. Opposite this on the south wall hang the colours of the United States Marine Corps which were laid up in the church in 1946. The USMC and the Royal

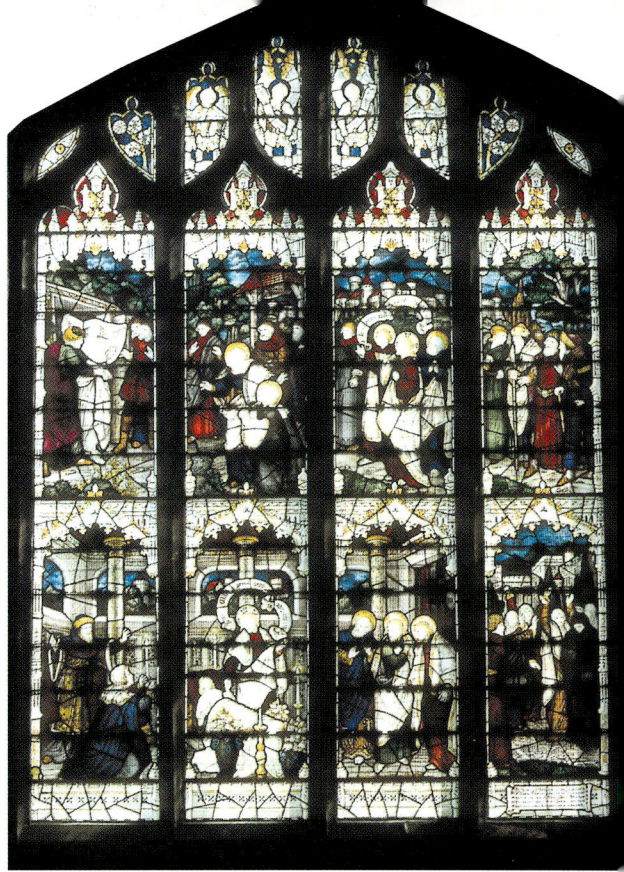

*The Strachan Window in the south aisle, designed by Kempe and executed by Kempe & Tower. Kempe's windows are marked with a small wheatsheaf while those of his nephew, Walter Ernest Tower, are marked with a small black tower.*

Welch Fusiliers have been closely linked since they served together in Peking (Beijing) in 1900.

## The Tower

The tower was built in the 16th century in the Perpendicular style. It is 45m (147ft) high and the lower level has a vaulted ribbed ceiling. For many years, the Royal Welch Fusiliers Chapel was located here and, consequently, many of their memorials are to be seen on the walls.

The west window was dedicated in 1895 to the Officers and Men of the Royal Welch Fusiliers. It was designed and installed by Messrs Clayton & Bell of London. The images in the glass include St David (the patron saint of Wales), St Deiniol and Edward, Prince of Wales, 'The Black Prince'. Below it is the west door which is enclosed by a 19th century oak panelled inner porch.

On the south and north walls are a number of brass plaques to noted members of the Royal Welch Fusiliers including Major General Sir Luke O'Connor who gained

*The restored pre-1643 font.*

the Regiment's first Victoria Cross at the Battle of the River Alma in 1854, and Lt. Colonel Doughty-Wylie who gained a Victoria Cross at Gallipoli in 1915. Two other plaques record those Fusiliers who fell in Waziristan (1920–23) and Cyprus (1958). On the south wall is a large marble memorial, decorated with two figures of Royal Welch Fusiliers with reversed arms which records the names of all members of the regiment killed in South Africa 1899–1902 and China 1900. This was unveiled by the Prince of Wales in May, 1903. Hanging from the walls are RWF colours and the colours of regimental organisations. Above the colours, on the north wall, are faint traces of a wall painting. The grotesques in each corner of the ceiling are also worthy of notice.

A spiral staircase, not normally accessible to the public, leads to the ringing room and, above that the bell chamber which houses ten bells. Higher still, the staircase gives access to the top of the tower which is surmounted by a battlemented parapet, four corner turrets and sixteen pinnacles. Each pinnacle is decorated with human faces from various periods of the tower's history, a fascinating chronicle from the dawn of the modern age to the 19th century. It seems likely that the stonemasons were given a free hand with decorating these pinnacles and took the faces around them as models. In addition there are some less than human faces perhaps representing the darker side of 16th century beliefs.

Externally, the tower is a fascinating structure but, unfortunately, much detail has been lost through the action of weathering and pollution on the soft sandstone. It can perhaps best be described by examining each face in turn.

The north wall, in addition to several decorative grotesques, has a number of statues, the lower of which represents St James the Great, patron saint of Spain and travellers. This may have been placed here as the Parish Church is on a routeway west–east from Wales to England and north-south through the Marches. This would have made it a convenient stopping place for travellers or it may have been in celebration of the marriage of King Henry VIII to Catherine of Aragon in 1509. Immediately above St James is a statue of St Giles flanked on either side by a king (possibly the young Henry VIII) and St John the Baptist. Above these, at the level of the clock is a statue of St Peter (left) and St Andrew (right). The centre figure has not been identified nor have the three figures in the upper row on a level with the belfry

The west wall is dominated by the west window. Below it and slightly to the right, is the stone placed here, close to the tomb of Elihu Yale, by Yale University in 1918.

The west door is decorated with the Tudor emblems of the rose and the portcullis (decorative features that also appear inside the church in a number of locations). Above the west window is a statue of St Barbara, the patron saint of towers, flanked by two crowned, but unidentified females. Immediately below the clock face is a statue of St Mary and the infant Jesus flanked by two figures on crutches (possibly St Giles, the patron saint of cripples). Finally, above the clock and between the louvres of the belfry, there are three more statues. Those on the left and in the centre are unidentified but that on the right is believed to be St Lawrence.

The east wall has only one identified statue, that of St Catherine, which appears on the left of the lower row. On her left shoulder is the representation of the wheel on which she was killed. As already mentioned, the tower of the 14th century church collapsed on St Catherine's day and her image may have been placed here to protect the tower or alternatively, it may have been chosen in recognition of Catherine of Aragon.

*Image of St Giles on the north face of the tower.*

*Facing: The west window.*

*Nine of the ten bells of St Giles photographed on the ground in 1955.*

The south side has many niches but there is no evidence that any statues were ever placed here.

The fabric of the tower underwent a major restoration between 1987 and 1991 at a cost of over £500,000. It was well described by the architectural historian Edward Hubbard: 'The crustaceous richness has a character of its own, and the recessed pinnacles continue the diminution of outline provided by the buttresses, giving a craggy, organic quality, with a marvellous feeling of strength'.

## Music in the Parish Church

St Giles is a living, working church, used daily for services and individual quiet prayer and contemplation. Throughout its history, the church has been a centre for music, whether it is the peal of bells carrying across the surrounding area, the magnificence of church organ music or the sound of voices raised in joy and celebration from both the choir and the congregation.

### The Bells

The earliest record of bells in St Giles notes a single bell donated by Deicws ap Madog of 'Llwyn y Cnottiau' in the early 15th century. In 1675, a bell that had formerly hung in St Asaph Cathedral was given to Wrexham in exchange for three smaller bells. The oldest bell still used in the church today is the Parson's Bell (or Five Minute Bell) which is rung before every service and which was donated in 1673.

A peal of ten new bells was cast by Abraham Rudhall of Gloucester, one of the finest bell-founders of the time, in 1726–7 at a cost of £294. They were transported up the river Severn to Shrewsbury and then by road to Wrexham. These are hung on a 5.18m (17ft) square frame and range in weight from 1270kg (25cwt) down to 254kg (5cwt). The bells were hoisted into the bell chamber by way of a hole which is visible in the vaulted ceiling of the base of the west tower, concealed by a painting of the Creation by the children of St Gile's School. Today, Wrexham is one of very few churches to have a complete ring of Rudhall's bells.

### The Organ

The original organ, once referred to as 'Ye fayrest organes in Europe' was destroyed in 1643 by soldiers of the Parliamentary army. The use of the plural 'organes' would suggest that it had two sets of keys. It stood in the rood loft above the east end of the nave. In 1629, the organist was Richard Deane. The next organ appears to have been installed in 1779 and was built by Green of London at a cost of over £378. It was located in the new gallery in the ante-nave. The first organist was probably John Gerrard who died in 1788 and he was succeeded by Edward Randles, the famous blind harpist and father of the infant progidy Elizabeth Randles. The organ gallery was moved under the tower in the 1820s and a new organ was built by Bewsher and Fleetwood of Liverpool. The organ gallery was re-constructed in 1851 to expose the west window.

The present organ, described as 'a masterpiece' and 'a remarkable instrument', was built in 1894 by Foster and Andrews of Hull at a cost